21st Century
Basic Skills
Library

BABY ZOO ANIMALS
HIPPOPOTAMUSES

by Katie Marsico

Cherry Lake Publishing • Ann Arbor, Michigan

3

Published in the United States of America
by Cherry Lake Publishing
Ann Arbor, Michigan
www.cherrylakepublishing.com

Content Adviser: Dr. Stephen S. Ditchkoff, Professor of Wildlife Sciences, Auburn University, Auburn, Alabama

Photo Credits: Cover and page 1, ©Flavijus/Dreamstime.com; page 4, ©Uryadnikov Sergey/Shutterstock, Inc.; pages 6, 14, and 20, ©Henk Bentlage/Shutterstock, Inc.; page 8, ©Yairleibovich/Dreamstime.com; page 10, ©Melissa Schalke/Dreamstime.com; page 12, ©Chatchai Somwat/Dreamstime.com; page 16, ©Lianquan Yu/Dreamstime.com; page 18, ©Nilanjan Bhattacharya/Dreamstime.com

Library of Congress Cataloging-in-Publication Data
Marsico, Katie, 1980–
  Hippopotamuses / by Katie Marsico.
    p. cm. — (21st century basic skills library) (Baby zoo animals)
  Includes bibliographical references and index.
  ISBN 978-1-61080-458-5 (lib. bdg.) — ISBN 978-1-61080-545-2 (e-book) — ISBN 978-1-61080-632-9 (pbk.)
1. Hippopotamidae—Infancy—Juvenile literature. 2. Zoo animals—Infancy—Juvenile literature. I. Title.
  SF408.6.H57M37 2013
  599.63'5—dc23   2012001729

Cherry Lake Publishing would like to acknowledge
the work of The Partnership for 21st Century Skills.
Please visit www.21stcenturyskills.org for more information.

Printed in the United States of America
Corporate Graphics Inc.
July 2012
CLFA11

TABLE OF CONTENTS

Bigger Than Human Babies

Hippopotamuses are huge **mammals**. They love being in the water!

They live in Africa.

Hippos are also found in zoos around the world.

A baby hippo is called a **calf**.

Hippos have one calf at a time.

Mother hippos are called cows.

Hippo calves weigh up to 100 pounds (45 kilograms).

They are ten times the size of most human babies!

A Hippo's Day

Hippo calves and their mothers are most active at night.

During the day, they try to keep cool. They rest in pools of water at the zoo.

Hippos mainly eat grass.

Zookeepers also feed them hay and grains. They also like apples, carrots, and **kale**.

A calf drinks its mother's milk for 8 months after birth.

Mother hippos are extremely **protective** of their calves.

A mother sometimes carries her baby. The baby lies on her back as she moves through deep water.

Zookeepers hear mother and baby hippos **communicate**.

Cows make low, short sounds called grunts. Grunts warn their babies of danger.

Welcoming New Calves

Wild hippos stay with their mothers for about 8 years.

They stay together for more or less time at zoos.

Calves are adults when they are about 8 years old. Then they can start having their own calves.

Then the zoo becomes home to new baby hippos!

Find Out More

BOOK

Shea, Therese. *Twenty Fun Facts About Hippos*. New York: Gareth Stevens Publishing, 2012.

WEB SITE

National Geographic Kids—Hippopotamuses
http://kids.nationalgeographic.com/kids/animals/creaturefeature/hippopotamus
Visit this site to watch a video about hippos, as well as to view photos and send an e-card.

Glossary

calf (KAF) baby of certain animals, such as hippos

communicate (kuh-MYOO-ni-kate) share information, ideas, or feelings

hippopotamuses (hih-poh-PAH-tuh-mus-iz) large mammals that live in Africa and spend much of their time in water

kale (KAYL) a type of cabbage

mammals (MA-muhlz) warm-blooded animals that have hair or fur, give birth to live babies, and make milk to feed their young

protective (pruh-TEK-tiv) careful to keep someone or something from harm

zookeepers (ZOO-kee-purz) workers who take care of animals at zoos

Home and School Connection

Use this list of words from the book to help your child become a better reader. Word games and writing activities can help beginning readers reinforce literacy skills.

a	called	have	live	own	times
about	calves	having	love	pools	to
active	can	hay	low	pounds	together
adults	carries	hear	mainly	protective	try
Africa	carrots	her	make	rest	up
after	communicate	hippo	mammals	she	warn
also	cool	hippopotamuses	milk	short	water
and	cows	hippo's	months	size	weigh
apples	danger	hippos	more	sometimes	welcoming
are	day	home	most	sounds	when
around	deep	huge	mother	start	wild
as	drinks	human	mother's	stay	with
at	during	in	mothers	ten	world
babies	eat	is	moves	than	years
baby	extremely	its	new	the	zoo
back	feed	kale	night	their	zookeepers
becomes	for	keep	of	them	zoos
being	found	kilogram	old	then	
bigger	grains	less	on	they	
birth	grass	lies	one	through	
calf	grunts	like	or	time	

Fast Facts

Habitat: Grasslands, in and around rivers, lakes, and swamps
Range: Africa
Average Length: 9.5 to 14 feet (2.9 to 4.2 meters)
Average Weight: 5,000 to 8,000 pounds (2,268 to 3,629 kilogram.
Life Span: About 40 years

Index

About the Author

Katie Marsico is the author of more than 100 children's and young-adult reference books. She has watched hippos and their babies at the zoo but hopes to never get too close to them in the wild.